CONRAD GREBEL'S PROGRAMMATIC LETTERS OF 1524

CONRAD GREBEL'S

PROGRAMMATIC LETTERS OF 1524

WITH FACSIMILES OF THE ORIGINAL GERMAN SCRIPT OF GREBEL'S LETTERS

Transcribed and Translated by

J. C. WENGER

Professor of Historical Theology
Goshen Biblical Seminary

HERALD PRESS
Scottdale, Pennsylvania 15683

Dedicated to

DEAN HANS RUDOLF VON GREBEL

Pastor of the Great Minster

Zürich, Switzerland

A lineal descendant of the

thirteenth generation from

CONRAD GREBEL

Dean H. R. v. Grebel

CONTENTS

INTRODUCTION

Conrad Grebel, the scion of a wealthy and prominent patrician family of Zürich, Switzerland, was born about 1498, and was educated in the Zürich Latin school called the Carolina, and in the universities of Basel (1514-15), Vienna (1515-18), and Paris (1518-20). He had also intended to pursue his humanist studies at the University of Pisa in Italy, but two factors caused him to drop the plan: (1) In 1521 he had an affair with a Zürich girl named Barbara, whom he married on February 6, 1522, and who bore him three children: Theophilus, 1522; Joshua, 1523; and Rachel, 1525. (2) In 1522 Grebel was brightly converted to an evangelical faith through his close association with the Swiss reformer, Huldrych Zwingli (1484-1531). Grebel immediately threw himself into the reform program of Zwingli with great energy, deep joy, and high hope. By the fall of 1523, however, Grebel began to grow critical of Zwingli for what appeared to him to be a rather lukewarm program of church reform, a program which, Grebel thought, looked too much to the powerful Zürich Council for the actualization of the Zwinglian hope of a German evangelical state church in northern Switzerland. By the fall of 1524 relations between Grebel and Zwingli were approaching the breaking point.

In 1523 Grebel had accepted Zwingli's teaching that children were saved by Christ and His redemptive work on Golgotha, and needed no ceremony to "seal" salvation to them. Grebel had also come to the conclusion that New Testament ecclesiology demanded a Free Church, dissociated from the state, and standing only on the Word of God and the Spirit of God. Grebel had also concluded that disciples of the Prince of Peace could under no circumstances resort to violence and killing. He was also al-

9

most fiercely devoted to the great Reformation principle of *sola scriptura*--that the Bible and the Bible alone is the norm of Christian doctrine and practice. Grebel's attitudes, particularly his rejection of infant baptism and of the magistracy, were a source of anguish for Zwingli. He made earnest efforts to bring Grebel and his tiny band of followers (less than twenty) to a less radical point of view. The climax followed the Great Disputation held before the Zürich Council on Tuesday, January 17, 1525. At this disputation Grebel pleaded his conviction that the New Testament demanded the baptism of believers only, and refused to recognize the jurisdiction of the Zürich Council in matters of faith. Zwingli, however, was by this time minded to retain the baptism of infants, and was also ready to defer to the Council on the tempo of the Swiss reformation. At the end of the disputation the Council ruled that Zwingli had demonstrated that there was nothing wrong with infant baptism. The next day the Council threatened with exile anyone who would fail to have his infants baptized. On Saturday, January 21, 1525, the Council further ruled that Grebel and his colleague, Felix Manz, must desist from holding any further lay Bible study meetings.

What should Grebel do? That night he and his friends met in a private home in Zürich, probably the home of the mother of Manz, to seek the mind of God through counsel and prayer, in this dire extremity. A feeling of fear fell upon the group and they knelt in fervent prayer. Following the prayer, a most amazing scene transpired. A priest, George of the House of Jacob (but commonly known by his nickname, Blaurock), knelt before Grebel requesting believer's baptism! Grebel complied. Whereupon, the others came to George, asking him for baptism! Thus arose the

first modern Free Church! (In the late fourth century, A.D. 380, Christianity had been made the official religion of both the Eastern and Western Empires by the joint edicts of Theodosius and Gratianus.) Later the Hutterites (1528) and the Amish (1693) separated from these so-called "Baptists" (*Täufer* in German). In the long run the *Täufer* came to be known as Mennists, Mennonists, and Mennonites, although officially still known as *Taufgesinnten* in Switzerland and *Doopsgezinden* in the Netherlands.

As the opposition of Zwingli and the Council to the *Täufer* grew more intense, Grebel and his colleagues reached out eager hands imploring help in various quarters. Earnest letters were sent to Luther, to Carlstadt, and to Thomas Müntzer. The 1524 letters of Grebel and his friends to Müntzer are easily the most significant of the extant products of Grebel's pen. It is true that these young Swiss dissenters from Zwingli knew almost nothing of Müntzer beyond what they gathered from his two tracts of 1524: *True Christian Faith and Baptism,* and *Spurious Faith.* They did learn with deep anxiety that Müntzer was perhaps thinking of taking the sword in his Saxon reformation. Thereupon Grebel reached for his pen and drafted these letters to Müntzer, the author of the two impressive tracts. But when the messenger who carried the letters arrived at Allstedt, Müntzer had left the city, and the only course of action evident to the messenger was to bring the letter back to Zürich. Grebel died of the plague at 28, the summer of 1526, at Maienfeld, and his brother-in-law Vadian must have saved the letter, for it is preserved to this day in the *Stadtbibliothek (Vadiana)* of St. Gall, Switzerland, under the signatures XI, 97 and II, 204. It was reproduced for this publication by Dr. Theres Maurer of that library, whose kindness is hereby gratefully acknowledged. The letters consist of six leaves, twelve pages: the first letter occupies seven full pages, with the eighth page having the last thirteen lines plus the address--which is written at a right angle to the thirteen lines. The second letter is on the fifth leaf, pages nine and ten, while the address is written on the outside of the sixth leaf which is otherwise blank. Including margins the pages measure approximately 8 1/2 x 12 3/4 inches. The letters are written in a fine hand, sharp and clear. Instead of commas, Grebel employs diagonals. For the facsimile reproductions of this book the margins were trimmed off, so that the writing would not need to be reduced in size, and each page was cut horizontally in half.

Previous German editions of these letters include C. A. Cornelius, 1860; Christian Neff, 1925; H. Boehmer and Paul Kirn 1931; L. von Muralt and W. Schmid, 1952; and Heinold Fast, 1962. English translations were published by Walter Rauschenbusch, 1905, and by George H. Williams, 1957 (a revision of the Rauschenbusch translation).

I carefully transcribed the German original, numbered the lines both of the German original and of the transcription, and translated the letters into English. I inserted a sort of rough indication of the lines of the German original in my English translation, although this cannot be exact because of the differing word order of the English translation. Elizabeth Horsch Bender, Assistant Professor of German Emeritus in Goshen College, • checked the translation and made a number of helpful corrections. It was her late husband, Dean Harold S. Bender, who authored the definitive biography of Grebel, 1950.

The perusal of the Bender biography reveals the deep convictions and yearnings of Conrad Grebel in 1524: (1) to set up a biblical church forthwith; (2) to see this church governed only by the Word of God and the Spirit of God; (3) to make a complete separation of church and state: that is, Grebel demanded a Free Church; (4) to assume the obligation to evangelize society--for the masses indicate by their lives that they are not regenerated disciples of Jesus Christ; (5) to call upon all men to repent, to believe on Christ, and to seal their covenant of discipleship by water baptism (Grebel and his followers generally baptized by affusion); (6) to practice a scriptural church discipline, that is, to insist that all church members strive earnestly to make the ethical standards of their lives conform to the New Testament; (7) to teach the people of God to live by "suffering love," renouncing force and violence in human relations, rejecting military service, and even refusing to serve as a magistrate; and (8) to render careful obedience to the New Testament--and this meant for the Swiss Brethren the rejection of the civil oath in conformity to the word of Christ.

These letters of 1524 set forth many of the above emphases of Grebel: *sola scriptura;* a Lord's Supper without [liturgical] singing, one which follows the explicit directives of Christ; a plain meetinghouse with nothing which could lead to a veneration of "sacred objects"--even such items as tablets containing the Ten Commandments; brotherly discipline according to Matthew 18; strict nonresistance, and a readiness to take up the cross of discipleship; the baptism of converted disciples of Christ; the saved status of children; and finally the painful anticipation that Zwingli will incite the persecution of his dissident followers. On only one point did the young reformer strike an unsound

note: in his earnest concern that the public worship of God is for
the glorious ministry of the Word, Grebel argued tediously and
at length against singing. In this untenable position, he was un-
critically following Zwingli. In fairness to Grebel, we must of
course remind ourselves that the only singing he was familiar
with was liturgical singing in Latin, not the congregational singing of a later day. Nothing in his experience had opened his eyes
to the possibility of inspiring and uplifting congregational sing-
ing--which all branches of the Continental Reformation ultimate-
ly realized: Lutheran, Reformed, and Anabaptist-Mennonite.
Indeed, many of the first-generation Swiss Anabaptists, even
colleagues of Grebel, became hymn writers.

The "false sparing" to which Grebel so often alludes, and
which he sharply rebukes, meant the unworthy diminishing of
the demands which Christ made upon His followers for total
obedience, cross-bearing, and discipleship. The Reformers, Grebel
felt, did a disservice to the gospel by not setting up a church
which was wholly obedient to the Word of Christ.

It is hoped that in the near future all of Grebel's 70 extant
letters (most of them stemming from his humanist years) can be
published. Perhaps it will also be possible to reissue the 1950
biography of Grebel written by Bender. Meanwhile, may these
letters of 1524 serve to portray the vision of this youthful reformer who is recognized as their first leader by a half-million
Mennonites around the globe, as well as a teacher of many of
the basic principles of the great Baptist Church of our day.

Goshen Biblical Seminary   J. C. WENGER
Goshen, Indiana 46526

October 18, 1968

CONRAD GREBELS PROGRAMMATISCHE BRIEFE VON 1524

CONRAD GREBEL'S PROGRAMMATIC LETTERS OF 1524

(The 345 lines of the two letters are numbered in this book, both in the original German, and its transcription, and in the translation.)

Frid gnad barmhertzigkeit von Gott unsserem vatter und Iesu Christo
unserem herren sy mit unss allen Amen. Lieber bruder Toman lass
dich umm gotz willen nit wunderen / dass wir dich ansprechend on titel / und
wie ein brůder ursachend hinfür mit unss zehandlen durch gschrift / und
5   dass wir ungefordert und dir unbekant / habend gedörfen ein gmein künftig
gsprech ufrichten. Gottes sun Iesus Christus der sich aller deren die do selig
werden söllend / einigen meister und houpt dar bütt / und unss brüdere
heisst sin / durch dass einig gmein wort allen brüderen und gleubigen /
hand unss getriben und betzwungen früntschaft und brůderschaft zemachen
10   und nachgende artikel antzetzeigen / Zů dem hat unss ouch din schriben
zweier büchlinen von dem erdichten glouben geursacht / darumb so wellist
ess im besten verstan umm Christi unsers heilands willen / sol unss ob got will zů gůtem
dienen und würken werden Amen. Wie nach dem unssere altforderen
von dem waren got / und erkantnuss Iesu Christi und dess rechtgschafnen
15   gloubens in in / und von dem waren einigen gmeinen götlichen wort / von
den götlichen brüchen Christenlicher liebe und wäsen abgefallen sind / on gott
gsatz und Evangelio in menschlichen unnützen unchristlichen brüchen und
Ceremonien gelebt und darinn selikeit zeerlangen vermeint habend / und
aber wit gefelt worden ist / wie dass die Evangelischen prediger antzeigt
20   habend und noch antzeigend zum teil / also ouch ietzund wil iederman in
glichsendem glouben selig werden / on frücht dess gloubens / on touff der versůchung
und probierung / on liebe / und hoffnung / on rechte Christenliche brüch / und
beliben in allem altem wäsen eigner lasteren / und gmeinen Ceremonischen
Endkristlichen brüchen touff und nachtmal Christi / in verachtung dess götlichen
25   worts in achtung dess bepstlichen / und dess wortess der widerbepstlichen

[1] May peace, grace, and mercy from God our Father and Jesus Christ [2] our Lord be with us all, Amen. Dear Brother Thomas, [3] For God's sake do not marvel that we address you without title and [4] as a brother request you to correspond with us, and that we have ventured [5] without your asking, and unknown to you, to [6] initiate dialogue. God's Son, Jesus Christ, who presents Himself as the one Master and Head of all those who [7] are to be saved, and who [8] calls us brethren through the one common word to all brethren and believers, [9] has moved and constrained us to establish friendship and brotherhood [with you] and to call your attention to the [10] following articles. Your writing of [11] two booklets on spurious faith also moved us to write to you. Therefore may you receive it [12] favorably for the sake of Christ our Savior, and if God wills, it shall also [13] serve and work for our good. Amen. Just as our ancient forefathers fell away [14] from the true God and from the knowledge of Jesus Christ, and from true [15] faith in Him, and from the one true, common, divine Word, and from [16] the divine rites of Christian love and being, and lived without God's [17] law and gospel in human, unprofitable, and unchristian rites and [18] ceremonies, and thought that thereby they would obtain salvation, and [19] yet fell far short of it, as the evangelical preachers have pointed out, [20] and are still in part pointing out, so also today everybody wants to be saved by a [21] make-believe faith, without faith's fruits, without the baptism of trial and [22] testing, without love and hope, without proper Christian rites, and while [23] continuing in the old blasphemous way of life, and in the common ceremonial, [24] antichristian rites of baptism and Christ's Supper: thus despising the divine [25] Word and following the papal word as well as the word of

prediger so ouch dem götlichen nit glich und gmess ist / in ansechung der
personen / und allerley verfürung wird schwarlicher und schädlicher geirret
dann von anfang der welt ie geschechen sy. Im semlicher irrung
sind ouch wir gewäsen die wil wir allein zůhörer und läser warend
30   der Evangelischen predigeren / welche an disem allem schuldig sind / uss
verdienst unserer sünden. Nach dem wir aber die gschrift ouch zehand
gnommen habend / und von allerley artiklen besechen / sind wir etwass bericht
worden und habend den grossen und schädlichen mangel der hirten / ouch
unseren erfunden dass wir got nit täglich ernstlich mit stettem sünftzen
35   bittend / dass wir uss der zerstörung alles götlichen wäsens und uss
menschlichen grewlen gefürt werdind / in rechten glouben und brüch
gottes kummind. In semlichem allem bringt dass faltsch schonen / die
verschwigung und vermischung dess götlichen wortes mit dem menschlichen
Ia sprechend wir ess bringt allen schaden / und macht alle götliche
40   ding hinderstellig / bedarf nit underscheidens und ertzellens. In dem
so wir semlichs merkend und beklagend / wirt zů unss gebracht
din schriben wider den falschen glouben und Touff / sind wir nach
bass bericht worden und befestet / und unss wunderbarlich erfreuwt dass
wir einen funden habend / der einss gmeinen christenlichen verstands mit
45   unss sy / und den Evangelischen predigeren / iren mangel antzeigen dörfe wie
sy in allen houpt artiklen falsch schonind und handlind / und eigens gůt dunken
ia ouch dess Endkristen über gott und wider gott setzind nit wie gesanten
von gott zehandlen und predigen zů stat Darumb so bittend und erma
nend wir dich alss ein brůder / by dem namen kraft wort geist und heil
50   so allen christen durch Iesum Christum unsseren meyster und seligmacher

the antipapal [26] preachers which is not identical with nor in agreement with the divine Word. In respect of [27] persons and all sorts of seduction we are in more dangerous and damaging error [28] than ever existed from the beginning of the world. In this same error [29] we too had been, as long as we were hearers and readers of [30] the evangelical preachers, who are guilty for all of this, in [31] recompense for our sins. But after we took the Scripture in hand, and [32] examined all sorts of items, we gained some insight and became aware of [33] the great and damaging deficiency of our shepherds and of [34] ourselves: that is, that we do not daily, earnestly, and with continuing sighs [35] cry to God that we might be led out of the destruction of all godliness of life and out of [36] human abominations, and that we might enter into true faith and [37] God's rites. In all this, the false sparing makes the divine Word [38] silent and mixes the human with it. [39] Yes, we claim that it damages everything and sets back all [40] things divine. To specify and elaborate is not necessary. While we were [41] taking note of and lamenting these things [42] your writing against spurious faith and baptism was brought to us, and we were more fully [43] informed and confirmed. It made us wonderfully happy to have found [44] one who was one with us in a common Christian understanding, and who ventured to point out to the [45] evangelical preachers their deficiency: how [46] in all the major articles [of faith] they practice false sparing, and follow their own notions, [47] yes, even those of Antichrist, above God and contrary to God, as is not right for ambassadors [48] of God so to act and so to preach. We therefore entreat and admonish [49] you as a brother, by the name, power, Word, Spirit, and salvation which [50] all Christians receive through Jesus

begegnet / wellist dich ernstlich flissen allein götlichs wort unerschroken
predigen / allein götliche brüch uffrichten und schirmen / allein gůtt
und recht schetzen dass in heiterer clarer gschrift erfunden mag werden /
alle anschläg / wort / brüch und gůtdunken aller menschen ouch din selbss /
55 verwerfen / hassen und verflüchen/. Wir verstand und hand gesehen dass /
du die mess vertütschet hast / und nüwe tütsche gsang uffgericht /
mag nit gůt sin / wann wir findet in dem nüwen Testament kein ler
von singen / kein bispil / paulus schilt die Corinthischen gelerten me
dann er sy rüme darumm dass sy in der gmein murmletend / glich alss
60 ob sy sungind / wie die Iuden und Itali ire ding pronuncierend in gsangs wiss.
Zum andren die wil dass gsang in latinischer sprach on götliche ler und
apostolisches bispil und bruch erwachsen ist / und nüt gůtz gebracht
nach gebuwen hat / wirt ess nach fil minder buwen in tütsch / und
ein usserlichen schinenden glouben machen. Zum dritten so doch paulus
65 garnach heiter dass gsang verbütt im 5 zun Ephesieren und im
.3. zun Colosseren die wil er sagt und lert man söll sich bereden
und ein andren underrichten mit psalmen / und geistlichen liederen /
und so man singen well / sol man im hertzen singen / und danksagen.
Zum .4. wass wir nit gelert werdend mit claren sprüchen und bispilen
70 sol unss alss wol verbotten sin alss stünd ess gschriben dass tů nit
sing nit Zum .5. Christus heisst sine botten allein dass wort uss predigen
in altem garnach / und nüwem Testament / paulus ouch also dass
die red Christi nit gsang under unss wone / der übel sing hat
ein verdruss / der ess wol kan ein hoffart. Zum .6. sol man nit
75 tůn wass unss gůt dunkt / zů dem wort und darvon nüt setzen / Zum .7.

18

Christ our Master and Savior, [51] to seek earnestly to preach only the divine Word, and unafraid, [52] to set up and defend only divine rites, to [53] esteem as right and good only what is found in crystal-clear Scripture, to reject, hate, and curse [54] all proposals, words, rites, and opinions of all men, even your own. [55] We understand and have noted that you have translated [56] the mass into German, and have begun to use German hymnody. [57] That cannot be right, when we find no teaching in the New Testament [58] about singing, and no example of singing. Paul scolds the learned at Corinth [59] more than he praises them because they chanted in the church service, [60] just as if singing, as the Jews and Italians pronounce their words in a singsong manner. [61] Second, since singing in the Latin tongue arose without divine teaching and [62] apostolic precedent and practice, and neither resulted in good [63] nor brought edification, it will much less edify in German, but will result in [64] an outward make-believe faith. Third, Paul quite [65] explicitly forbids singing in Ephesians 5 and [66] Colossians 3, when he teaches that they shall teach and admonish [67] one another with psalms and spiritual songs, [68] and if anyone wishes to sing, he shall sing and give thanks in his heart. [69] Fourth, that which is not taught by clear instruction and example [70] we shall regard as forbidden to us--just as if it stood written, Do not do this; [71] do not sing. Fifth, the only command Christ gave His ambassadors [72] in the Old [Testament] was to preach the Word; the same in the New. Paul likewise commands that [73] the Word of Christ shall dwell in us, not singing. He who sings poorly [74] is vexed; he who is able to sing well becomes conceited. Sixth, a person is not to do [75] what seems right to him; it is the Word which we are to follow,

wilt du die mess abtůn můss nit mit tütschem gsang geschechen /
dass din ratschlag fillicht oder von dem Luther her ist [8] sy můss
mit dem wort und uffsatz Christi uss gerüttet werdend
.9. dann sy ist nit von got gepflantzet .10. dass nachtmal der vereim
80 barung hat Christus uffgesetzt / und pflantzet .11. die wort so Mathei
26 . Marci .14. Luca .22. und .1. Cor. 11.sollend allein gebrucht werden
weder minder noch me / [12] der diener uss der gmein solte sy vorsprechen /
uss einem der Evangelisten oder uss paulo .13. sind wort dess uffgesetzten
malss der vereimbarung / nit der consecrierung .14. ess sol ein gmein
85 brot sin / on götzen und zů satz .15. wann es bringt ein glichsenden
andacht / und anbettung dess brotes / und ein abtzug von dem innerlichen
Ess sol ouch ein gmein trinkgschirr sin .16. diesses wurd die anbettung
abtůn und recht erkantnuss und verstand dess nachtmalss bringen / die wil
dass brot nüt anderss ist dann brot / im glouben der lib Christi / und ein
90 inlibung mit Christo / und den brüderen / wann im geist und liebe můss
mann essen und trinken wie Io. im 6 ca. und in den andren antzeigt
paulus so im .10. und .11. zum Corinthieren / actuum .2. clar erlernet
wirdt. 17. ob ess wol nun brott ist so gloub und brůderliche liebe
vorgat sol ess mit freud genommen werden / wann so manss bruchte in der gmein
95 solt ess unss antzeigen dass wir warlich ein brott und lib / und ware
brüder mitteinander werind und sin weltind etc .18. So einer aber
sich funde nit brůderlichen mögen läben isst er zů der verdamnuss
wann er isst on underscheid wie einander mal / und schendt die liebe dass
inner band / und dass brott dass usser .19. wann ess ermant in ouch

20   100 nit an den lib und blůt Christi dess Testamentes an dem Crütz / dass

with no additions. Seventh, [76] if you wish to abolish the mass, do not introduce German singing. [77] That is perhaps your idea, or it originated with Luther. [78] [Eighth], by the word and counsel of Christ it must be rooted out. [79] Ninth, [Singing in the meeting] was not established by God. Tenth, the Supper of unity [80] was set up by Christ and established by Him. 11. Only the words of Matthew 26, [81] Mark 14, Luke 22, and 1 Corinthians 11 shall be used: [82] no more and no less. 12. The minister of the congregation shall pronounce them, [83] reading from one of the Gospels or Paul. 13. They are the words of institution of the [84] Supper of unity, not of consecration. 14. Common [85] bread shall be used, with no idolatry and with no additions: for these [human additions] introduce a make-believe [86] reverence and adoration of the bread, as well as a turning away from the inward. [87] Also a common drinking vessel shall be used. 16. This will [88] eliminate the adoration, and guarantee a true knowledge and understanding of the Supper. For [89] the bread is simply bread, yet by faith the body of Christ, and an [90] incorporation into the body of Christ and with the brethren. One must [91] eat and drink in the Spirit and in love, as John 6 and elsewhere indicate, as [92] Paul points out in 1 Corinthians 10 and 11, and as Acts 2 clearly teaches. [93] 17. Although it is simply bread, where faith and brotherly love [94] prevail it shall be partaken of with joy. When observed in that way in the congregation [95] it shall signify to us that we are truly one loaf and one body, and that we are and intend to be true [96] brothers one with another. 18. But if one should be [97] found who is not minded to live the brotherly life, [98] he eats to his condemnation, for he does not discern the difference from another meal. He brings shame on the [99] inward bond, which is love, and on the bread, which is the outward bond. 19. For he fails to be instructed [100] as to the body and blood of Christ and the Testament He made on the cross, that he

er umm umm [sic] Christi und der brüderen dess houptes und glideren
willen / läben und liden well .20. ess solt ouch nit von dir
ministriert werden / darmit gieng die mess ab / dass einig essen / wann
dass nachtmal ist ein antzeigung der vereimbarung / nit ein mess und

105 Sacrament darumm sol ess nieman allein bruchen / weder im todbett nach
sunst dass brott soll ouch nit verschlossen werden etc uff ein einige
person / wann niemantz soll im selbss dass brott der vereimbarten nemmen
allein / er sye dann mit sim selbss uneiss / dass ist keiner etc 21. ess
soll ouch nit gebrucht werden in templen nach aller gschrift und gschicht

110 wann ess bringt ein falschen andacht .22. ess solt offt und fil gebrucht
werden .23. solt nit on die regel Christi Mathei im xviij gebrucht
werden / wolaber ess ist ie nit dess Herren nachtmal / wann on die selb
so louft iederman nach dem usseren dass inner die liebe lasst man
farren / gand brüder und falschbrüder hinzů / oder essendss 24.

115 so du ess ie zůdienen wilt woltend wir ess gschech on pfäffische kleidung
und messgwand / on gsang on zůsatz
25. der zitt halb wüssend wir dass Christus den apostlen im nachtmal
geben und die Corinthier ouch also gebrucht hand . bestimmend by unss
kein gwisse tzit / etc darmit nach dem du dess nachtmalss dess herren

120 fil bass bericht bist / und wir allein unseren verstand antzeigend / sind wir nit
recht dran / ler unss dass besser / und wellist dass gsang und mess lassen fallen
und alles allein nach dem wort handlen und brüch der apostlen herfür tragen
mit dem wort / und uffrichten / mag ess nit sin so were ess besser man
liesse alle ding latin beliben und ungeendret und gemitlet / mag dass recht

125 nit uffgericht werden / so ministrier ouch nit nach dinem oder dess Entchristen

shall live and suffer [101] for the sake of Christ and the brethren, the Head and the members of Christ. [102] 20. Also, it should not be administered by you [sacerdotally]. [103] That is how the mass originated, namely, individual participation, whereas [104] the Supper is an exhibition of unity. It is not a mass nor a [105] sacrament. Therefore no one shall receive it alone, neither on a deathbed nor [106] otherwise. Neither shall the bread be locked up, etc., for the use of an individual [107] person, and no one shall take for his own individual use the bread of those in unity-- [108] unless he is not in unity with himself, which is never the case with anybody, etc. 21. It [109] shall also not be used in temples, according to all the Scriptures, and what we learn from history, [110] for that is what creates a false adoration. 22. It shall be observed often and much. [111] 23. It shall not be observed except in conformity with Christ's rule in Matthew 18, [112] for then it would not be the Lord's Supper, for without Matthew 18 [113] everyone runs after the outward, and that which is inward, namely, love, one lets go; [114] and brethren and false brethren go to the Supper together and eat. 24. [115] When you wish to serve [communion], we would desire that you do so without priestly clothing [116] and the vestments of the mass, without [liturgical] singing and without additions.

[117] 25. As to the time, we know that Christ gave it to the apostles at supper time, [118] and that the Corinthians so observed it. Yet we do not designate [119] any specific time, etc. We know that you are [120] far better instructed about the Supper of the Lord than we are; we only indicate our understanding. If we are not [121] right about this, instruct us better. But do drop the singing and the mass [122] and operate only according to the Word, and draw and establish from the Word the rites of the apostles. [123] If that cannot be done it were better just to [124] leave everything remain in Latin, unchanged, and mediated [by priests]. If that which is right [125] cannot be set up, do not admin-

pfäffischen bruch / und ler zemintsten wie ess sin solt alss Christus Ioannis
im vj tůt / und lert wie man sin fleisch und blůt essen und trinken můss
und sicht nit an den abfal / oder dass widerkristlich schonen so die aller glertisten
erste Euangelische prediger / ein waren abgott. uffgericht und in alle welt
130 gepflantzet hand / Ess ist fil weger dass wenig recht bericht werdind durch
dass wort gottes recht gloubind / und wandlind in tugenden und brüchen /
denn dass fil uss vermischter ler falsch hinderlistig gloubind / Wie wol
wir dich manind und bettend / hoffend wir doch du tüest ess selbss / und
manend ouch darumm aller liebist dass du unserem brůder also früntlich
135 geloset / und bekent hast dich ouch etwass zu fil nachgelassen haben. und
dass du mitsampt Carolostadio by unss für die reinisten usskünder und
prediger dess reinisten götlichen wortes geacht sind / und üch beden so ir
sy straffend und billich / die menschen wort und brüch mit götlichen vermischend
sollend ir üch billig von der pfaffheit pfründen und allerley nüwen und
140 alten brüchen / eignen und alten gůtdunken von rissen und gar rein werden.
Sind üwer pfründ gestifft uff zins und zehenden bede warem wůcher
wie by unss / und so nit ein gantze gmein üch ertzücht wellind ir üch der
pfründen entzüchen / ir wüssend wol wie ein hirt ernert werden sol. Wir
versehend unss fil gůtz zů Iacobo Struss und anderen etlichen die wenig
145 geacht werdend by den hinlessigen gschriftgelerten und doctoren zů wittemberg.
wir sind ouch also verworfen gegen und von unseren gelerten hirten
ess hangt inenn alle mentschen an schaft dass sy ein sündigen süssen Chr'um [Christum]
predigend / und inen gůtz underscheids gebrist wie du in dinen bůchlinen
antzeigst / die unss armgeistigen fast über die mass gelert und gesterkt
24
150 hand / und sind also aller dingen glich on dass wir mit leid vernommen

ister it either according to your own custom or that of the antichristian [126] priests. At least teach how it ought to be, as Christ does in John [127] 6, teaching how a person must eat and drink His flesh and blood. [128] He pays no attention to the apostasy nor to the antichristian sparing--like the most learned and [129] outstanding evangelical preachers do, making the Supper an actual idol which they have set up and [130] established in the whole world. It is far preferable that a few be rightly instructed in [131] the Word of God, believing aright, walking in virtues, and observing [biblical] rites [132] than that many through adulterated doctrine falsely and deceitfully "believe." Although we [133] admonish and entreat you, yet we do hope that you will of yourself wish so to act. [134] We give this admonition the more freely because you listened to our brother in such a friendly manner, [135] also acknowledging to him that you too have given way a bit too much, also because we regard [136] you and Carlstadt as the purest proclaimers [137] and preachers of the purest Word of God. And if you both [138] justly rebuke those who mix human words and rites with the divine, [139] you really ought also to dissociate yourselves from the priesthood, benefices, and all sorts of new and [140] old usages, and from all other notions, both your own and those which are ancient, and thereby become entirely sound. [141] If your benefices, like ours, are founded on tithes and interest, both of which are simply usury, [142] and you are not supported by the whole congregation, you ought to [143] withdraw from the benefices. You know well enough how a shepherd ought to be supported. We [144] anticipate much that is good from Jacob Strauss and several others who are [145] little esteemed by the negligent scribes and doctors at Wittenberg. [146] We also are rejected by our learned shepherds. [147] All men cling to them because they preach a sinful sweet Christ, [148] and they lack the power to discern, as you point out in your booklets [149]--which have richly instructed and strengthened us, who are poor in spirit. [150] We stand together on everything, except that we learn with sorrow [151] that you

25

hand wie du taflen uffgericht habist / so wir kein gschrift noch bispil
in den nüwen Testament finden In dem alten solt ess wol usserlich
geschriben werden ietz aber in dem nüwen sol ess in die fleischin
taflen dess hertzen geschriben werden / wie die verglichung beder
155 Testamenten usswist wie wir durch paulum 2 Cor. 3 . hieremiam im 31 .
capitel im 8 zun hebreieren / Ezechiels im 36 . bericht werdend
so wir nit irrend / alss wir nit meinend und gloubend / wellist die Taflen
wider zegrund richten / ess ist uss eignem gůtdunken erwachsen / ein vergebli
cher kost der do zůnemmen wurd / und gantz abgötist werden und sich in
160 alle welt inpflantzen wie mit den götzen gschehen ist / ess machte ouch ein
argwon alss ob ie etwass usserlichs an der statt der götzen darab der unglert
leren künde / stan und uffgricht werden müste / so allein dass usserlich
wort gebrucht soll werden / nach aller gschrift bispil und gebott wie
fürnemlich 1 Cor. xiiij . und Col . 3 . unss angetzeigt wird / semliche
165 erlernung uss dem einigen wort / möcht mit der zitt etwas hinderstellig
werden / und ob ess ie kein schaden bringen wurd so welte ich ie nüt
nüwes erfinden und uffrichten / und den hinlessigen / falsch schonenden
verfürenden glerten nit nachfolgen oder glich sin / uss eignem gůtdunken
nit ein einigs stuk erfinden leren und uffrichten . Züch mit dem wort
170 und mach ein Christenliche gmein mit hilf Christi und siner Regel
wie wir sy ingesetzt findend mathei im xviij und gebrucht in den
Epistlen / leg ernst ann und gmeinss gebett und abbruch nach dem
glouben und der liebe one gebott und ungetzwungen / so wirdt
gott dir und dinen schäflinen zů aller luterkeit helfen wirt dass gsang
175 und taflen fallen Ess ist wissheit und rates me dann gnůg in der

26

have erected tablets [in the church building], when [152] the New Testament teaches nothing of the kind, neither by text or example. In the Old Testament, to be sure, [153] the writing was indeed outward, but now in the New the writing is to be on the fleshy [154] tablets of the heart. This is confirmed by a comparison of the two [155] Testaments. See Paul in 2 Corinthians 3, Jeremiah 31, [156] Hebrews 8, and Ezekiel 36: where this is taught. [157] Unless we are mistaken, which we do not think or believe, you should again do away with the tablets. [158] This arose out of your own notions, but is a futile [159] expense, however, and is bound to increase and become utterly idolatrous--and spread into the [160] whole world, as did the idols. It will also give rise to the [161] notion that always something external has to be set up, in place of the idols, by which the unlearned [162] might learn. But it is the outward [163] Word alone which is to be used, according to the example and command of the whole Scripture, [164] especially as pointed out to us in 1 Corinthians 14 and Colossians 3. But this kind of [165] learning from the one Word [likely the Ten Commandments on the tablets] might in the course of time become inferior. [166] And even if it never would do any harm, yet I would never invent and set up [167] anything new, and thereby follow and become like the negligent, falsely sparing, learned ones [168] who lead others astray; nor would I from my own notions invent, teach, and set up [169] a single item. Press forward with the Word and [170] create a Christian church with the help of Christ and His Rule [171] as we find it instituted in Matthew 18 and practiced in the [172] epistles. Apply it with earnestness and common prayer and restraint, in line with [173] faith and love, and without law and compulsion. Then [174] God will bring you and your lambs to full soundness, and the singing [175] and tablets will be abolished. There is

gschrift wie man all stend alle menschen leren regieren wisen und
fromm machen soll welcher sich nit besseren nit glouben wil / und
dem wort und hendlen gottes widerstrebt / und also verhart den
sol man nach dem im Christus und sin wort sin regel geprediget / und
180 er ermanet wirt mit den drien zügen und der gmein / den sprechen
wir uss gottess wort bericht sol man nit tötten / sunder ein heiden und
zoller achten und sin lassen / man soll ouch dass Evangelium und sine annnemer
nit schirmen mit dem schwert oder sy sich selbss / alss wir durch unseren
brücher [sic] vernommen hand dich also meinen und halten . Rechte gleubige
185 Christen / sind schaff mitten under den wölfen / schaff der
schlachtung / müssend in angst und nott trübsal ferfolgung liden und
sterben getoufft werden / in dem für probiert werden / und dass vatterland
der ewigen růw nit mit erwürgung liplicher finden / sunder der
geistlichen erlangen Sy gebruchend ouch weder weltlichs schwert
190 nach krieg / wann by inen ist dass tötten gar abgetan wol aber
wit werend noch dess alten gsatztes in welchem ouch (so fer wir unss bedenkend)
der krieg nach dem sy dass gelobt land eroberet hattend / nun ein plag ge/
wesen ist / von dem nit me . dess Touffs halb gfalt unss din schriben wol
begerend ouch witer bericht werden von dir / wir werdend bericht dass man
195 on die regel christi dess bindens und entbindens / ouch ein erwachsner nit
gtoufft solte werden / Den touff beschribt unss die gschrift / dass er bedütte
durch den glouben und das blůt Christi (dem getoufften dass gmüt enderendem
und dem gloubenden vor und nach) die sünd abgewaschen sin / dass er bedütte dass man
abgstorben sie und sölle der sünd / und wandlen in nüwe dess läbens
200 und geist / und dass man gwüss selig werd so man durch den inneren touff

28

more than enough wisdom and counsel in the [176] Scripture, how all classes and all men shall be taught, governed, instructed, and [177] made God-fearing. Whoever will not repent and believe, but resists [178] the Word and the moving of God, and so persists [in sin], [179] after Christ and His Word and Rule have been preached to him, and [180] he has been admonished in the company of the three witnesses and the congregation, such a man, we declare, [181] on the basis of God's Word, shall not be killed, but regarded as a heathen and [182] publican, and let alone. One should also [183] not protect the gospel and its adherents with the sword, nor themselves. We learn from our [184] brother that this is also what you believe and hold to. True believing [185] Christians are sheep among wolves, sheep for the [186] slaughter. They must be baptized in anxiety, distress, affliction, persecution, suffering, and [187] death. They must pass through the probation of fire, and reach the Fatherland [188] of eternal rest, not by slaying their bodily [enemies] but by mortifying their [189] spiritual enemies. They employ neither worldly sword [190] nor war, since with them killing is absolutely renounced. Indeed they do [191] not defend themselves after the manner of the old law—in which (so far as we understand) [192] war was, after the promised land had been conquered, only a plague. [193] Of this, no further comment. On the subject of baptism we are really pleased with your book, and we [194] desire further instruction from you. We understand that even an adult is not to be baptized [195] apart from Christ's rule of binding and loosing. [196] Scripture describes baptism for us as signifying that [197] through faith and the blood of Christ our sins are washed away: to the one baptized that his inner self has been changed, and that he [198] believes, both before and afterward. It signifies that one should be and is [199] dead to sin, and walking in newness of life [200] and spirit; also that he shall certainly be saved by the inward bap-

den glouben / nach der bedütnuss läbe / also dass / dass wasser den glouben
nit befeste und mere wie die glerten zů Wittemberg sagend und wie er
ser fast tröste / und die letst zůflucht in dem todbett sye . Ite dass ess
ouch nit selig mache wie augustino Tertullianus Theophylactus und

205 Ciprianuss zů schmach dem glouben und liden Christi an den alten erwachsnen
zů schmach dem liden Christi an den ungetoufften kindlinen / gelert ha/
bend Wirt haltend uss nach gemelten gschriften Gene . 8 . Deute . 1 .
30 . 31 . und . 1 . Cor . 14 . Sapientia . 12 . Ite 1 petri . 2 . Ro. 1.2.7.10.
mathei . 18 . 19 . marci . 9 . 10 . Luca .18 etc dass die alle kind die noch

210 nit zů underscheid dess wüssens gůtts und böss kummen sind / und von dem boum dess
wussens nach nit geessen habend / dass sy gwüss selig werdind durch dass
liden Christi dess nüwen adams welcher inen dass verschimpft läben
widergebracht hab / die wil sy allein dem tod und verdamnuss underwor/
fen gsin werind wo Christus nit gelitten hett / nach nit erwachsen zů dem prästen der zerbrochnen

215 natur / man künne unss denn bewisen dass Christus nit für die kind gelitten
hab . dass man aber fürwirft der gloub werd von allen erforderet
so da selig werden söllind / schlüssend wir die kind uss und haltend
sy on glouben selig werden und nit glouben uss obgemelten sprüchen
Und beschlüssend uss beschribung dess Touffs / und uss den gschichten

220 (nach welchen kein kind getoufft worden ist) ouch uss den obgemelten
sprüchen so allein von allem handel der kinden luttend / und andere
alle gschrift die kind nit betrift) dass der kindertouff ein unsinniger
gotzlesteriger grewel sy wider alle gschrift ouch wider dass bapstumm
wan wir findend dass fil Iar nach der apostlen zitt durch Ciprianum

225 und augustinum sechss hundert Iar lang gloubende and ungloubende

tism [201] if he lives his faith according to this significance. But the water does [202] not strengthen nor increase faith--as the learned ones at Wittenberg say--and that it gives [203] very great comfort, and is even one's final refuge on one's deathbed! Furthermore, it does [204] not save, as Augustine, Tertullian, Theophylact, and [205] Cyprian taught: and by such teaching they brought faith and the suffering of Christ to shame, in relation to adults; and also in relation to the unbaptized infants they [206] brought shame upon the suffering of Christ. On the basis of the following Scriptures [207] we hold that all children who have not yet come [210] to the discernment of the knowledge of good and evil, and who have not yet eaten of the tree of [211] knowledge, are certainly saved through the [212] suffering of Christ: Genesis 8, Deuteronomy 1, [208] 30, 31, 1 Corinthians 14, Wisdom 12, 1 Peter 2, Romans 1, 2, 7, 10, [209] Matthew 18, 19, Mark 9, 10. Christ is the [212] New Adam who [213] has restored their ruined life, for they would have been subject to death and damnation only [214] if Christ had not died. Also, they have not yet grown up to the infirmity of our broken [215] nature--unless indeed we could be shown that Christ did not suffer for the children! [216] But if the objection is raised that faith is demanded of all [217] who are to be saved, we exclude children from this requirement, holding that [218] they are saved without faith. We hold this on the basis of the Scriptures cited above, and [219] from the description of baptism, also from the historical accounts [220] (according to which no child was baptized). From the above [221] Scriptures (which alone apply to the whole subject of children, and [222] all other Scriptures [demanding faith] do not apply to children), we conclude that infant baptism is a senseless, [223] blasphemous abomination, contrary to all Scripture. Indeed it is contrary even to the papacy, [224] for we learn through Cyprian and Augustine that for many years after the time of the apostles, even for [225] six hundred years, believers and unbelievers were [226] baptized together,

mitteinandren getoufft sind worden etc die wil du semlichs alss zehen malen
bass bekenst und wider den kindertouff dine protestationes heruss gelassen
hast verhoffend wir du handlist nit wider dass ewig wort wissheit
und gebott gottes nach welchen man allein gloubende touffen soll und

230 touffist keine kind . Ob du oder Carolostadius nit gnůgsam wider den
kindertouff schriben werdend / mit aller zůgehört / wie und warumb
man Touffen sölle etc So wirde ich min heil versůchen (Cůnrat Grebel)
und dass ich angehebt han sollen uss schriben wider all so biss har (on dich) von dem
touff verfürlich und wüssenlich schribend / und die unsinnig

235 gotzlesterig form dess kindertouffs tütsch hand / alss Luter . Löw.
osiander / und die Strassburger / und ouch etliche noch schantlicher ge/
handlet hand . ob ess von gott nit gewendt wirt so bin und wird
ich mitsampt unss allen der verfolgung gwüsser sin von den glerten etc
dann anderen lütten . Wir bittend dich wellist allte brüch der endchristy

240 nit bruchen ouch nit nemmen / alss Sacrament . Mess . Zeichen . etc
Allein an dem wort halten und schalten wie allen gesanten / und dir
und Carolostadio foruss wol anstat (und ir mer tůnd weder alle predican
ten aller nationen Halt unss für dine brüder und verstand dises unser
schriben von grosser freuden und hoffnung zů üch durch gott) wegen

245 beschehen / und ermann tröst und sterke unss wie du wol kanst / bitt
gott den herren für unss dass er unserem glouben zehilf kumme
wann wir gern glouben weltind / und so unss gott ouch zebetten verlicht
wellend wir ouch für dich und alle bitten dass wir alle nach unserem
brůf und stand wandlind dass verlich unss gott durch Iesum Christum

250 unseren Heiland amen Grütz unss alle brüder die hirten und schäfli

32

etc. Since you know this ten times [227] better than we, and have published your protests against infant baptism, [228] we hope that you are not acting against the eternal Word, wisdom, [229] and commandment of God (according to which only believers are to be baptized) [230] by baptizing a single child. If you or Carlstadt do not write sufficiently against [231] infant baptism, and all that is associated with it, how and why [232] one is to baptize, etc., I (Conrad Grebel) will try my hand at it. [233] I have already begun to write against all those (except yourself) who hitherto have written misleadingly and willfully on [234] baptism, and who have translated into German the senseless and [235] blasphemous liturgy for infant baptism—such as Luther, Loew, [236] Osiander, and those of Strassburg; and some have been even more shameful. [237] Unless God avert it, [238] I and my colleagues are more certain to suffer persecution from the learned ones [239] than from other people. We entreat you not to use nor adopt the old antichristian rites, [240] such as sacrament, mass, signs, etc. [241] Hold to the Word alone, and rebuke as ambassadors should, especially you [242] and Carlstadt, for you are doing more than all the preachers of [243] all nations. Count us as your brethren, and take this our [244] letter as our confident expression of great joy and hope toward you through God. [245] Exhort, comfort, and strengthen us, as you are well able to. Pray [246] God the Lord for us that He may come to the aid of our faith, [247] for we do desire to believe. And as God enables us to pray [248] we will also intercede for you and for all, that we may all walk according to our [249] calling and state. God grant us this through Jesus Christ [250] our Savior. Amen. Greet for us all

so dass wort dess gloubens und heilss mit begird und hunger annemmend
etc Noch einss wir begerend din widerschriben und so du etwass
ussgan lassist / unss durch disen botten / und ander zůschikist So du und
Carolostadius einess gemütess sind begerend wir ouch bericht werden

255 wir hoffends und gloubendss / Diser bott so ouch dem lieben unserem
brůder Carolostadio brief gebracht hat von unss sye dir befolet .
und magst du zů Carolostadio kummen / dass ir mitt einandren
antwurtind / wurd unss ein hertzliche freud sin der bott soll wider
zů unss kummen / wass wir imm nit gnůgsam belonet habend / wirt

260 in siner widerfart ersetzt werden .   Gott sye mit unss
          Wass wir nit recht verstanden habend berichte
                    und lere unss
          Datum zů Zürich uff den fünften tag Herbstmonets Im Mvᶜ und
                    xxiiij Iar

265 Cůnrat Grebel . anderess kastelberg . felix Mantz . Hanss Oggenfüss .
Bartlime pur . Heinrich aberli . und andere din brüder ob got wil
in Christo die semlichs zů dir verschriben habend / wünschend dir
und unss allen / und dinen schaflinen allen / biss uff andere botschaft
dass war wort gottes waren glouben liebe und hoffnung mit allem frid

270 und gnad von gott durch Christum Iesum Amen .
          dem luter hab ich C. Grebel in unser aller namen schriben wellen
          und manen abtzeston von dem schonen / so er on gschrift brucht
          und in die welt / und ander nach im gepflantzet hand so hat
          ess min trübsal und zit nit mögen zůgäben . Ir tůnd ess

34   275 nach üwer pflicht etc

the brethren, the shepherds and the sheep, who receive [251] the word of faith and salvation with desire and hunger, [252] etc. One thing more. We are eager for a reply from you. And if you [253] publish anything, send it to us with this messenger or others. We are also eager to learn whether you and [254] Carlstadt are of one mind. [255] We hope and believe that you are. We commend to you this messenger, who has also transmitted letters from us to our beloved [256] brother Carlstadt. And if you should [257] visit Carlstadt, and you could jointly [258] reply, it would afford us hearty joy. The messenger plans to return [259] to us. Whatever we have not adequately paid him will be made up [260] at his return.

God be with us!

[261] Whatever we have not rightly understood,

inform [262] and instruct us.

[263] [264] Zürich, September 5, 1524.

[265] Conrad Grebel, Andrew Castelberg, Felix Manz, John Ockenfuss, [266] Bartholomew Pur, Henry Aberly, and others of your brethren [267] in Christ, if God will, who joined in writing this to you, wish for you [268] and all of us, until we write again, [269] the true Word of God, and true faith, love, and hope, with all peace [270] and grace from God through Christ Jesus. Amen.

[271] It was my intention (C. Grebel) to write to Luther in the name of all of us, [272] and to exhort him to desist from his policy of sparing, which he and others who followed him, without the support of Scripture, introduced [273] in the world. But [274] my affliction and time did not permit. You do it; [275] it is your duty, etc.

[On lower part of center section of the
last sheet, after folding twice, is the
address:]

Dem wahrhaftigen und getrü
wen verkündiger dess Evange/
lij Tomas Müntzer zů altstett
am hartz unserem getrüwen
und lieben mitbrůder in
          Christo etc

[On lower center on back
of last sheet, after
folding twice:]

To the true and faithful
Proclaimer of the Gospel
Thomas Müntzer of Altstett
am Hartz, our true and
loving fellow-brother in
Christ, etc.

Hertzliebster brůder Toman Wie ich in unser aller namen geschriben hat in
die il und gmeint disser bott wurd nit harren dass wir dem Luther ouch schribind
also hat er regenss halb müssen beitten und harren do han ich für mich und die
anderen mine und dine brüder ouch dem Luter gschriben / und in gemanet abzestan
280 von dem falschen schonen der schwachen welche sy selbs sind / der Andress Castelberg
hat Carolostadio gschriben . In dem so kumpt Hansen Huiufen von Hall
hie unserem mitburger und mittbrůder / der by dir gewäsen ist im kurtzem / ein Brief
und schantlich büchlin dess Lutherss dass keinem zeschriben zůstatt der primitiae
wil sin wie die apostel . paulus lert anderss porro servum domini etc Ich sich
285 dass er dich an die achss gäben wil / und dem fürsten überantwurten / an welchen
er sin Evangelium gebunden hat alss aaron den Moysen für ein gott haben mŭsst
diner büchlin und protestationen halb so find ich dich on schuld / du verwerfist
dann den touff gar / kann ich nit daruss verstan / sunder dass du den kindertouff
und den unverstand dess Touffs verdamnest Wass dass wasser bedütte Ioannis . 3 .
290 wellend wir in diner und biblischer gschrift bass besechen . dess Huiufen
brŭder schribt du habest wider die fürsten geprediget dass man sy mit der
funst angriffen solte / ist ess war / oder so du krieg schirmen woltest / die taflen/
dass gsang / oder anderss so nit in clarem wort fundist / alss du disse gemelten
stuk nit findest So ermann ich dich by gmeinem heil unser allen wellist darvon
295 abstan und allem gůtdunken ietz und hernach / so wirst du gar rein werden
der unss sunst in andren artiklen bass gefalst den keiner in disem tütschen
ouch anderen länderen . So du dem Luther und hertzogen in die hend kumpst
lass die gmelten artikel fallen / und by den andren stand wie ein helde und
kempfer gottes / biss stark du hast die Bibel (daruss Luther Bibel bubel
300 babel macht) zů schirm wider das abgötisch Luterisch schonen dass er und

[276] Dearly beloved Brother Thomas: After I had written in the name of all of us, in [277] haste, thinking that the messenger would not wait until we had also written to Luther, the messenger was compelled to delay and wait because of [278] rain. And so I did write to Luther in my name, and in the name of [279] my brethren and yours, admonishing him to desist [280] from his false sparing of the weak--who are actually themselves! Andrew Castelberg [281] wrote to Carlstadt. In the meantime John Huiuff of Hall arrived [282] here, our fellow-citizen and fellow-brother, who was recently with you. He brought a letter [283] and a shameful booklet by Luther which is not appropriate for anyone to write [284] who wishes to be a top-level leader like the apostles. Paul teaches differently: "The servant of the Lord [must not strive]," etc. I perceive [285] that he wishes to put you to the ax, to deliver you over to the prince--to whom [286] he has bound his gospel, like Aaron had to have Moses as his god! [287] As to your booklets and protests, I find you guiltless. I do not understand you to be rejecting [288] baptism as such, but you condemn infant baptism [289] and the misunderstanding of baptism. What "water" means in John 3 [290] we will carefully examine in your book and in the Scripture. The [291] brother of Huiuff writes that you preached that the princes should be attacked with [292] violence. Is that true? If you wish to defend war, the tablets, [293] the singing, or other things which you do not find in express words [of Scripture]--as you do not find the [294] points mentioned--I admonish you by the common salvation of us all that you [295] desist from all notions of your own both now and henceforth. Then you will be completely sound, [296] for in the articles [of the faith] you please us better than anyone else in this German country [297] and in other countries. If you should fall into the hands of Luther and the duke, [298] drop the articles mentioned, but stand by the others like a hero and [299] warrior of God. Be strong! You have the Bible (of which Luther has made bubel [villainy] and [300] Babel [either the O.T. Babel, or chatter]) for your defense against the idolatrous sparing of Luther (which he

die glerten hirten by unss in alle welt gepflantzet hand / wider den
hinderlistigen hinlessigen glouben / wider ire predigung darinn sy den Christum
nit lerend wie sy soltend / und aller welt eben dass Evangelium uffgetan
habend dass sy ess selbss läsind oder läsen soltind / aber nit filen wann iederman hangt an inen.

305 by unss sind nit zwentzig die dem wort gottes gloubind / nun den personen
Zwingli / Löwen / und andren so anderschwo sind glert geachtet . Und ob du
darumb liden müsstest / weist wol dass ess nit anderss mag sin Christus müss
noch mer liden in sinen glideren er aber wirt sy sterken und fest erhalten biss
zů dem End / Gott geb dir und unss gnad . Wann unsere hirten sind ouch

310 also grimm und wüttend wider unss scheltend unss bůben an offenlicher
Cantzel und Satanas in angelos lucis conversos / wir werden ouch mit der zitt sächen die verfolgung
über unss gan darumm so bitt für unss by gott . Noch ein mal manend wir   [durch sy
dich / und dass darumm / dass wir dich umm der clarheit willen diness wortes
also hertzlich liebend und achtend / und vertruwt zů dir getörend schriben

315 wellist nichts nach menschlichem gůtdunken eignem oder frembdem handlen
leren oder uffrichten / was uffgericht ist widerumm niderwerfen / und wellist
allein götlichs claress wort und brüch / mitsampt der Regel Christi / unver /
mischtem Touff und unvermischtem nachtmal / wie wir in dem erstem brief
angerůrt habend / und du bass bericht bist dann unser hundert / uffrichten

320 und leren etc Wann so du und Carolostadius / Iacobuss struss / und Michel
Stifel nit gar rein zeflissen sin woltind (alss ich aber und mine brüder hoffend
ir werdinds tůn) were ess wol ein ellend Evangelium in die welt
kummen Ir aber sind wit reiner weder unsere hie und die zů Wittemberg
die uss einer gschriftverkerung in die ander / und uss der blindtheit in andre

325 grössere täglich fallend Ich gloub und halt dass sy ware bäpstler und

and [301] the learned shepherds in our area have introduced into the whole world), against the [302] deceitful, negligent faith, against their preaching in which they do [303] not teach Christ as they should. They have opened up the gospel for the whole world [304] that they can read it for themselves (or should read it), but not many do, for everybody just relies on them. [305] With us there are not twenty who believe the Word of God. People only put their trust in persons like [306] Zwingli, Loew, and others who elsewhere are regarded as learned. And if you [307] have to suffer for it, you know well that it cannot be otherwise. Christ must [308] suffer still more in His members. But He will strengthen and preserve them steadfast, even [309] unto death. God give you and us grace! Our shepherds are so [310] furious and enraged against us that they rail at us from the [311] pulpit, calling us boys and Satans [disguised as] angels of light. We will also, in the course of time, see persecution come [312] upon us through them. Do therefore entreat God for us. Once more we admonish [313] you, and for the reason that [314] we warmly love and esteem you [313] for the soundness of your words, and hence write you with confidence. [315] Do not act, teach, or set up anything according to human notions, yours or that of others, [316] and that which is thus set up, abolish. Set up and teach [317] only the clear Word and rites of God, together with the Rule of Christ [Matthew 18], unadulterated [318] baptism and unadulterated [Lord's] Supper, as we [319] touched upon in our first letter to you--and on which you are better instructed than a hundred of us. [320] If you and Carlstadt and Jacob Strauss and Michael [321] Stiefel do not give diligence to be wholly sound (as I and my brethren, however, hope that [322] you men will) it will be a miserable gospel indeed which is come into the world. [323] But you are far more sound than our [scholars] here, and than those in Wittenberg, who fall [324] from one perversion of Scripture into another, and fall daily from one blindness into a still [325] worse blindness. I am actually convinced that they want to be

Bäpst werden wellind Ietz nit me Gott der hertzügen mit sinem sun
Iesu Christo unserem heiland / und sinem geist und wort sye mit dir und
unss allen . Cûnrat Grebel / andress Castelberg / felix mantz / Heinrich aberli
                    Ioannes Panicellus / hanss oggenfûss Hanss Huiuff
330   din lantzman von Hall dine brüder / und siben nüw
                    Iung müntzer dem Luther .
So dir fry nachgelassen wirt / witer zepredigen und nichts begegnet
wellend wir dir unssers schribens zů dem Luther Copy schiken und sin antwurt so er
unss widerschribt / wir habend in gemanet und unsere hie ouch / darmit
335   so ess gott nit hinderen wurde / wellend wir iren mangel antzeigen
und nit fürchten wass unss darumm begegnen werde / wir hand ouch sunst
kein Copy behalten denn allein dess briefs so wir zů Martino dinem wi/
dersächer geschriben habend / darumm vernimm unser unglert unbehowen
schriben zů guttem uff / und biss gwüss dass wirss uss warer liebe getan
340   habind / wann wir sind mit wort und anfechtung und widersächeren
glich / wie wol du bass gelert und sterker im geist . Umm diser glichförmige
willen habend wir gnůg mit dir gerett oder gschriben. Wellist unss
so ess gott haben wil dine Christen grüssen und allen gmeinklich in eim
langen brief widerschriben / wirst du unss grosse freud / und gemerete
345   liebe zů dir erweken .

genuine papists and [326] popes. No more now! God our Captain, with His Son [327] Jesus
Christ our Savior, and His Spirit and Word, be with you and with [328] us all.

       Conrad Grebel, Andrew Castelberg, Felix Manz, Henry Aberly, [329] John
       Panicellus (Broetli), John Ockenfuss, John Huiuff [330] your countryman of
       Hall, your brethren, and seven new [331] young "Müntzers" against Luther.
[332] If you are permitted to go on preaching, and nothing happens, [333] we will send you
a copy of our letter to Luther and his answer, if he [334] replies to us. We admonished him,
also our [pastors] here. [335] Unless God restrains, we will point out to them their lack,
[336] and not fear what may thereby come upon us. We have kept [337] no copy of any
letter except the one we wrote to Martin [Luther] your opponent. [338] Will you therefore accept kindly our unlearned and uncouth [339] letter; and be certain that we wrote in
true love. [340] For we are one [with you] in word and struggle and in opponents, [341] although you are more learned and stronger in spirit. Because of this similarity [342] we con-
versed with and wrote to you at length. [343] If God will, give our greetings to the Christians there, and unite in writing us all a [344] long letter. You will thereby afford us great
joy, and awaken in us increased [345] love for you.

[On bottom third of a cover sheet,
which was also folded twice, is
this address:]

Der brief gehört
ouch Toman Mün/
tzer zů

Zů altstetten
am Hartz

[On bottom third of cover
sheet, after folding twice:]

This letter belongs
also to Thomas Münt-
zer
    at Altstetten
        am Hartz

FACSIMILE

of the 1524 Grebel Letters

Sind gnad vnd barmherzikeit von Gott vnserem vatter vnd Jesu Christo
vnserem herren sy mit vns allen Amen. | Lieber bruder Toman loß
dich vm gotz willen nit wunderen / das wir dich ansprechend on titel / vnd
wie ein bruder vrsachend hinfür mit vns zehandlen durch gschrift / vnd

5   das wir vngefordert vnd dir vnbekant / habend gedörfen in gmein künftig
gsprech vfrichten. Gottes sun Jesus Christus der sich aller deren die do selig
werden söllend / einigen meister vnd houpt dar bütt / vnd vns brüdere
heisst sin / durch das einig gmein wort | allen brüderen v. glaubigen /
hand vns getriben vnd bezwungen fründschaft vnd bruderschaft zemachen

10   vnd nachgende artikel anzezeigen / Zu dem hat vns ouch dis schriben.
Zweier büchlinen von dem erdichten glouben vervrsacht / darumb so wellist
es im besten verstan vm Christi vnsers heilands willen / sol vns ob got wil zu gutem
dienen vnd würcken werden Amen. Wie nach dem vnsere altforderen
von dem waren got / vnd erkantnuß Jesu Christi vnd des rechtschafnen

15   gloubens in in / vnd von dem waren / einigen gmeinen göttlichen wort / von
den göttlichen büchen / Christenlicher liebe vnd wäsen abgefallen sind / on Gott
gsatz vnd Evangelio / vnd in menschlichen vnnützen vnchristlichen bruchen vnd
ceremonien gelebt vnd daim seligkeit zuerlangen vermeint habend / vnd
aber mit gefelt worden ist / wie vnd das die Evangelischen prediger angezeigt

20   habend vnd noch anzeigend / zum teil / also ouch ietzund wil iedermann in

...sendem glouben sech werden / on frücht deß gloubens / on touf der versůchung

und probierung / on liebe / und hoffnung / on rechte christenliche brüch / und

ſ beliben in allem altem wäsen eigner lasteren / und gmeinen ceremonischen

endchristlichen brüchen touf und nachtmal christi / in verachtung deß göttlichen

25 worts / in achtung deß bepstlichen / und deß worteß der widerbepstlichen

prediger so ouch dem göttlichē nit glich und gmeß ist / in ansehung der

personen / und allerley verfürung wirt schwarlicher und schädlicher geiret

dan von anfang der welt ie geschechen sy . In semlicher irrung

sind ouch wir gewäsen die wil wir allein zůhörer und läser warend

30 der evangelischen predigeren / welche an disem allem schuldig sind / vß

verdienst unserer sünden . Nach dem wir aber die gschrift ouch zehand

gnomen habend / und von allerley artiklen besehen / sind wir etwaß berücht

worden und habend den grossen und schädlichen mangel der hirten / ouch

unseren erfunden daß wir got nit täglich ernstlich mit stettem sünfzen

35 bittend / daß wir ... vß der zerstörung alles göttlichen wäsens und vß

mentschlichen gewalten gefürt werdind / in rechten glouben und brüch

gottes kumind In semlichem allem bringt daß falsche schonen / die

verschwigung und vermischung deß göttlichen worts mit dem mentschlichen

Da spricht   sprechend wir eß bringt allen schaden / vnd macht alle göttliche

40 ding hinderstellig / bedarf nit vnderscheidens vnd erzellens . In dem
so wir semlichs merkend vnd beklagend / wirt zů vnß hernß gebracht
Bin schriben wider den falschen glouben vnd ~~Couf~~ Couf / sind wir nach
baß bericht worden vnd befestet / vnd vnß vunderbarlich erfrewwt daß
wir einen funden habend / der vnß gmeinen christenlichen verstand mit

45 vnß sy / vnd den euangelischen predigern / iren mangel antzeigen dörfe wie
sy in allen houpt artiklen ~~falsch~~ schämind vnd handlind / vnd eigens gůt dunken
ja ouch deß endkristen über gott vnd wider gott setzind nit wie gesanten
von gott behandlen / vnd predigen zůstat   Darumb so bittend vnd erma
nend wir dich alß ein Bruder / by dem namen kraft wort geist vnd heil

50 so allen christen durch Jesum Christum vnseren meyster vnd seligmacher
Begegnet / wellist dich ernstlich flissen allein göttlichs wort mertzroken
predigen / allein göttliche bůch vschirhten vnd schirmen / allein gůtt
vnd recht schetzen daß in heiterer clarer geschrift erfunden mag werden /
alle anschläg / wort / bůch vnd gůtdunken aller menschen ouch din selbs

55 verwerfen / hassen vnd verfluchen /. Wir verstand vnd hand gesehen daß /
gsang. Du die meß vertütschet hast / vnd nüwe ~~tütsche~~ gsang vfgericht /
mag nit gůt sin / wann wir findet in dem nüwen Testament kein lee

51

von singen / Item Bispil /   paulus schilt die Corinthischen gelerten in
dem er sy unne darum daß sy in der gmein murmletend / glich alß
ob sy sungind / wie die Juden und Itali ire ding pronuncierend in gsangs wiß .
Zum andren die wil das gsang in latinischer sprach on göttliche ler und
apostolisches bispil und bruch erwachsen ist / und nit guts gedracht
nach gebuwen hat / wirt eß noch fil minder buwen in tütsch / und
ein ossterlichen schinenden glouben machen . Zum dritten so doch paulus
darnach heiter daß gsang verbütt im 5 zum Epheseren und im
.3. zum Colosseren die wil er sagt und leert man soll sich bereden
und ein andren underrichten mit psalmen / und geistlichen liederen /
und so man singen well / sol man im hertzen singen / und dankfagen .
Zum .4. waß wir nit gelert werdend mit claren sprüchen und bispilen
sol uns alß wol verbotten sin alß stünd eß geschriben / daß du nit
singen sollt. Zum .5. Christus. heißt sine botten allein das wort uß prediegen
in alem darnach / und nüwem Testament / paulus ouch also das
die red Christi nit gsang under uns werne / der übel singt hat
ein verdruß / der eß wol kan ein hoffart . Zum .6. sol man nit
tün waß uns gut dunckt / zu dem wort und darvon nit setzen / Zum .7.
wilt du die meß abtün muß nit mit tütschem gsang geschechen / so
daß din ratschlag villicht oder von dem Luther her ist / sy müß

52

mit dem wort und uffsatz Christi ~~erscheinr~~ ussgerüttet werdend

.9. Dann sy ist nit von got gepflantzet .10. Das nachtmal der verein-

80 barung hat Christus uffgesetzt / und pflantzet .11. Die wort so Matthei

26. marci .14. Luce .22. und .1.Cor.11. ~~#~~ sollend allein gebrucht werden

weder minder noch me / der diener uss der gmein solte sy vorsprechen /

uss einem der Evangelisten oder uss paulo .13. sind wort des uffgesetzten

mals der vereinbarung / mit der conferierung .14. es sol ein gmein

85 brot sin / on götzen und zusatz .15. dann es bringt ein abgschenden

und acht / und anbettung des brotes / und ein abzug von dem innerlichen

es sol auch ein gmein trinckgschirr sin .16. dises wurd die anbettung

abtün und recht erkantnuss / und verstand des nachtmals bringen / die wil

das brott nit anders ist dan brot / im glouben der lib Christi / und ein

90 inlibung mit Christo / und den brüderen / wann im geist und liebe muss

man essen und trincken wie so. im 6 ca. und in den andern anzeigt /

paulus im .10. und .11. zum Corinthieren / actum .2. clar erlernet

wirdt .17. ob es wol nun brott ist so gloub und brüderliche liebe

sol es

vorgat mit fruchd genomen werden / wann so mans bruchte in der gmein

95 solt es uns anzeigen das wir warlich ein brott hand lib / und ware

brüder miteinander weind und sin weltind ~~ec~~ .18. so einer aber

sich funde mit brüderlichen mögen laben ist er zu der verdamnuss

wan' er ißt on underscheid wie einander mal / und schendt die liebe | daß
inmer bamd / und daß brott daß eßer · 19 · wan eß ermant ... in ouch
100   mit an den lib und blut Christi deß Testamentß an dem Crütz / daß
er um ... um Christi wi und der brüderen deß houptß und gliderenn
willen / büßen und liden well · 20 · eß solt ouch nit von dir
ministriert werden / damit gieng die meß ab / daß einig essen / wan
daß nachtmal ist ein anzeygung der vereinbarung / nit ein meß und
105   Sacrament darum sol eß nieman allein brachen / weder im todbett nach
sunst f daß brott soll ouch nit verschlossen werden ... uff ein einige
person / wan niemantz soll im selbß daß brott der vereinbarten nemen
allein / er sye dan mit sim selbß unreiß / daß ist keiner ... 21 · eß
soll ouch nit gebrucht werden in templen nach aller gschrift und gschicht
110   wan eß bringt ein gfalschen andacht · 22 · eß solt offt und vil gebrucht
werden · 23 · solt nit / an die regel Christi Matthei im ... gebrucht
werden / wolaber eß ist ... nit deß herren nachtmal / wan an die selb
so louft iederman nach dem vßeren daß iner die liebe laßt man
faren / gand brüder und falschbrüder hinzů / oder essend ...
115   so du eß ... zůdienen wilt woltend wir eß gschech on pfäffische kleidung
und meßgwand / on gsang on zůsatz

.25. der zitt bald wüssend wir daß Christus den aposteln im nachtmal
geben und die Corinthier ouch also gebrucht hand.) bestimmend dy noch
kein gwüsse zit / wie ich   darmit nach dem du deß nachtmalß deß herren
fil baß bericht bist / und wir allein unseren verstand anzeigend / sind wir mit
recht dran / ler uch daß besser / und wellist daß gsang und meß lassen fallen
und alleß allein nach dem wort handlen und brüch der aposteln herfür tragen
mit dem wort / und verrichten / mag / eß nit sin soll / wer eß besser man
liesse alle ding latin beliben und ungeendret und vermittlet / mag daß recht
nit verricht werden / so ministrier ouch nit nach dinem oder deß endtchrists
pfäffischn bruch / und ler zeministen wie eß sin solt   alß Christus joannis
im vij tut / und lert wie man sin fleisch und blut essen und trinken müß
und sicht nit an den abfal / oder daß widerkristisch schonen so die aller gelertisten
echt evangelische prediger / im waren abgott verricht und in alle welt
gepflanzet hand / Eß ist fil weger daß wenig recht bericht werdind durch
daß wort gottes recht glondind / und wandlind in tugendn und brüchen /
den daß fil uß vermischter ler falsch hinderlistig glondind / wie wol /
wir dich manend und bettend / hoffend wir doch du tüst eß selbß / und
manend ouch darum aller liebst daß du unserem brüder / also früntlich
geloser / und bekent hast / ouch etwas / zu fil nachgelassen haben . und

55

daß ir mitsampt Carolostadio by vnß für die römisch schrifftkünder vnd
prediger deß reinsten göttlichen wortes geacht sind / vnd sich beden so ir
sÿ straffend vnd billich / die mensch en wort vnd brüch mit göttlichen vermischend
sollend iz üch billich / von der pfaffheit pfründen vnd allerleÿ nüwen vnd
alten brüchen / eignen vnd alten gütdunken von ziehen vnd gar rein werden .
Sind üwer pfründ gestifft vff zins vnd zehenden daß bede waren wücher
wie by vnß / vnd so nit ein gantze gemein üch erzücht wellend iz üch der
pfründen entzüchen / ir wüssend wol wie im hie ernert werden sol , wir
versehend vnd vnß fil gütz zů Jacobo Struß vnd anderen ettlichn die wenig
geacht werdend by den hinlessigen schrifftgelerten vnd Doctorn zů Wittemberg .
Wir sind ouch also verwoefen gegen vnd von vnseren gelerten herren
Jst es hangt inen alle menschen an schaft daß sy im sündigen süssen clam
predigend / vnd inen gütz vnderscheid gebrist wie du in dinen büchlinen
anzeigst / die vnß armgeistigen fast über die maß gelert vnd gesteckt
hand / vnd sind also aller dingen glich on daß wir mit leid vernomen
hand wie du taflen vffgericht habst / So wir kein schrifft noch beispil
in den nüwen Testament finden Jn dem alten solt es wol vsserlich
geschriben werden ich aber in dem nüwen sol eß in die fleischin
taflen deß hertzen geschriben werden / wie die verglichung beder

155 Testamentes schreibt wie wir durch paulum 2 Cor. 3. Hieremia im 31.
capitel im 8 Zun hebreeren / Ezechiels im 36. bericht werdend
so wir nit irrend / alß wir nit meinend vnd gloubend / welche die Tafflen
wider zegrund richten / eß ist vß eignen Gutdunken erwachßen / vm vergeb-
licher kost der do zünemen wurd / vnd gantz abgöttisch werden vnd sich in

160 alle welt impflantzen wie mit den götzen geschehen ist / eß machte ouch im
argwon alß ob sie ettwaß vsserlichs an der statt der götzen daraß der vnglert-
ten bünde / stan vnd vfgericht werden müste / so allein daß vsserlich
wort gebrucht soll werden / nach aller geschrift bispil vnd gebott wie
fürnemlich 1 Cor. xiiij. vnd Col. 3. vnß angezeigt wird / sömliche

165 erlernung vß dem einigen wort / möcht mit der zitt ettwaß hinderstellig
werden / vnd ob eß ie kein schaden bringe wurd so welte ich ie nüt
nüwes erfinden vnd vfrichten / vnd denen im hinlessigen pfalsch schonenden
verfürenden gleerten nit nachfolgen oder glich sin / vß eignem Gutdunken
nit ein einigs stuk erfinden leren vnd vfrichten. Suche mit dem wort

170 vnd nach ein christenliche gmein mit hilf Christi vnd siner Regel
wie wir sy ingesetzt findend Mathei im xviij. vnd gebrucht in den
Epistlen / leg ernst an vnd gmeinß gebett vnd abbruch nach dem

glouben vnd der liebe one .ß gebott vnd vngetzwungen / so wirdt
gott dir vnd dinen schäflinen zů aller luterkeit helfen wirt daß gsang
175 vnd taflen fallen Eß ist wißheit vnd rates me dan gnůg in der
gschrift wie man all stend alle menschen leren regieren wisen vnd
from machen soll welcher sich mit besseren mit glouben wil / vnd
dem wort vnd handlen gottes widerstrebt / vnd also verhart den
sol man nach dem im christus vnd sin wort sin regel geprediget / vnd
180 er ermanet wirt mit den dryen zügen vnd der gmein / den sprechend
wir uß gottes wort bericht sol man nit töten / sunder im heiden vnd
zöller achten vnd sin lassen / man soll ouch daß euangelium vnd sine annemer
nit schirmen mit dem schwert oder sy sich selbs / alß wir durch vnseren
bücher vernomen hand dich also meinen / vnd halten . Rechte gloubige
185 Christen / sind schaff vnd der so mitten vnder den wölfen / schaff der
schlachtung / müssend in angst vnd nott trübsal verfolgung liden vnd
sterben getoufft werden / in dem für probiert werden / vnd daß vatterland
der ewigen rüw nit mit erwürgung liplicher finden / sunder der
geistlichen erlangt werden . Sy gebruchend ouch weder weltlichs schwert
190 nach krieg / wan by inen ist daß töten gar abgeton wol aber

58

wit werend noch deß alten gsatztes in welchem ouch (so fer ~~~~ wir vnß~~~~ bedenkend)
der krieg nach dem sy daß gelobt land erobret haltend / mun im plag oc
wesen ist / von dem nit me . Deß Toufß halb gfalt vnß din schriben wol
begerend ouch witer bericht werden von dir / wir werdend bericht daß man

195 an die regel christi deß bindens vnd entbindens / ouch im erwachsner nit
getoufft solte werden / Den touff beschribt vnß die gschrift / daß er bedütte
durch den glouben vnd daß blůt Christi (dem getoufften daß gmůt enderendem
vnd gloubenden vor vnd nach) die sünd abgewäschen sin / daß er bedütte daß man
abstorben sie vnd sölleß der sünd / vnd wandlen in nüwe deß läbens

200 vnd geist / vnd daß man gwüß sälig werd so man durch den inneren touff
den glouben / nach der bedütnuß läbe / also daß daß wasser den glouben
nit befeste vnd mere wie die glerten zů Wittemberg sagend vnd wie er
ser fast tröste / vnd die letst zůflucht in dem todbett sye . Itt daß eß
ouch nit sälig mache wie Augustin Tertullianus Theophylactus vnd

205 Cyprianus zů schmach dem glouben vnd liden Christi an den alten er wachßnen
zů schmach dem liden Christi an den vngetoufften kindlinen / glert ha=
bend Wir haltend vß nach gemelten gschriften Gene. 8. Deute. 1.
30 . 31. vnd . 1. Cor. 14 . Sapientz 12 . . 1 petri . 2. Ro. 4 . 1. 2. 7. 10.

mathei 18. 19. marci 9. 10. Luce. 18. etc. Daß die alle kind die noch
nit zu underscheid deß wüssent gutts und böß kumen sind und von dem boum deß
wüssens nach nit gessen habend / daß sy gloubig selig werdend durch daß
liden Christi deß nüwens adams welcher inen daß verschimpft läben
widergebracht hab / die wil sy allein dem tod und verdamnuß underworffen
sind weilend sy nach nit erwachsen sind dem prästen der zerbrochnen
natur / man künde uns den bewisen daß Christus nit für die kind gelitten
hab. Daß man aber fürwircht der gloub werd von allen erforderet
so da selig werden söllind / schlüssend wir vß die kind vß und haltend
sy on glouben selig werden und nit glouben vß obgemelten sprüchen
und beschlüssend vß beschribung deß Toufs / und vß den geschichten
(nach welchen kein kind getoufft worden ist) ouch vß den obgemelten
sprüchen so allein von allem handel der kinder lutend / und andere
B: alle geschrift die kind nit betrift) Daß der kindertouff ein vnsiniger
vorbergiger gewalt sy wider alle geschrift ouch wider das bapstum
vom wir findend daß fil Jar nach der aposteln zeit durch Cyprianen
und augustinen sechshundert Jar lang gloubende und vngloubende

miteinandern getoufft sind worden etc. Die wil du semlichs alß zeher malen
daß bekenst vnd wider den Kindertouff dine protestationeß heruß gelassen
hast verhoffend wir du handlist mit wider das ewig wort wißheit
vnd gebott gottes nach welchem man allein glaubende touffe soll vnd
touffst keine Kind . Ob du oder Carolostadius mit gnugsam wider den

230

kindertouff schriben werdend / mit aller zugehört / wie vnd wenn
man Touffen sölle etc. So wirde ich min heil versuchen (Cůnrat Gredel)
vnd daß ich angehebt han wider alle so biß har (on dich) von dem
touff verfürlich vnd wüssenlich schribend / vnd die vnsinnig

235

vogleistung form deß kindertouffs tütscht hand / alß Luter . Lewo .
Oslander / vnd die Strßburger / vnd ouch etliche noch schantlicher ge
handlet hand . Ob eß von gott nit gewendt wirt so bin vnd wird /
ich mitsampt vnß allen der verfolgung gwüsser für von den glerten etc
dem anderen lütten . Wir bittend dich welliст alle brüch der endchrist

240

mit bruchen ouch nit nemen / alß Sacrament . Meß . zeichen etc
allein an dem wort halten vnd schalten wie allen gesanten / vnd die
vnd Carolostadio forus wol omstat / vnd iz mer tům weder alle p deren
ten aller nationen Halt vnß für dine Brüder vnd verstand dißeß vnßer
schriben von grosser freuden / vnd hoffnung zů üch durch gott) wechen

Vestchehen / und erhan tröst und stärke unß wie du wol kanst / bitt
gott den herren für unß / daß er unserem glouben zehilff kume
wan wir gern glouben weltind / und so unß gott ouch zebätten verlicht
wellend wir ouch für dich und alle bitten / daß wir alle nach unserem
brüff und stand wandlind das verlich unß gott durch Jesum Christum
unseren heiland amen Brüg unß alle brüder die hirten und schäffli
so das wort deß gloubens und heilß mit begird und hunger annemend
ich   Noch einß wir begerend din widerschribn und so du etwaß
usßgon lassist / unß durch disen botten / und ander zuschickst So du und
Carolostadius einß gemütß sind begerend wir ouch / bericht werden
wir hoffends und gloubends /. diser bott so ouch dem lieben unserem
Brüder Carolostadio brieff gebracht hat von unß fye die befolet /
und magst du zu Carolostadio kunden / daß ir unß mitt einandern
antburtind / und unß ein hertzliche frund sin der bott sol wider
zu unß kumen / waß wir im nit gnugsam belonet habend / wirt
in siner widerfart ersetzt werden .   Gott sye mit unß
              waß wir nit recht verstandy habend berichte
              und do lere unß /

Datt zů Zürich vff den fünften tag Herbstmonets Jm ᴐᴣ vᵗ vnd
xxiiij Jar

265 Cůnrat Grebel . Andereß Castelberg . felix Mantz . Hanß Oggenfůß
Bartlime puren . Heinrich aberli vnd andere vnßer brüder ì ob gott wil /
in Christo die ſemlichʒ ʒů dir verschribñ habend / wünſchend dir
vnd vnß allen / vnd dinen ſchäflinen allen / biß vff andere botſchaft
Daß war wort gotteß waren glouben liebe vnd hoffnung mit allem heil
270 vnd gnad von gott durch Christen Jeſum Amen .

Den Anter hab ich er C. Grebel in vnſer aller namen ſchriben wellñ
vnd manen abʒeston von dem ſchonen / ſo er an geſchrift brucht
vnd in die welt / vnd onder nach im gepflantʒet band ſo hat
eß mir redtſal vnd ʒit nit mögen ʒů ſchaffen . Je thůnd eß
275 nach üwer pflicht ꝛc

Dem warhaftigen vnd getru,
wen verkündiger deß euange,
liy Toma Müntzer zů altstett
am hartz vnßerem getrüwen
vnd lieben mitbrůder in
Christo roß

Hertzliebster Bruder Thoman wie ich in vnser aller namen geschriben hat in
die il vnd gemeint diser bott werd nit harren das wir dem Luther ouch schribind
also hat er regens halb müssen beitten vnd harren do han ich für mich vnd die
andere mine vnd dine bruder / ouch dem Luter geschriben / vnd in gemacht abzestan
von dem falschen schonen der schwachen welche sy selbs sind /   Der andreß Castelberg
hat Carolostadio geschriben /   In dem so kumpt hanßen hinßen wider von hall
hie vnser mitburger vnd mittbruder / der by dir gewäsen ist im kurtzem / ein brief
vnd schanklich büchlin des Luthers das keinē geschriben zustatt   der primitz
wil syn wie die apostel Paulus lert anderß porro serum domini rc /   Ich sich
das er dich an die achß gäben wil / vnd dem fürsten überantwurten / an welchen
er sin Euangelium gebunden hat alß aaron den Moysen für ein gott haben müßt
Diner büchlin vnd protestationen halb so find ich dich on schuld / du verwerfist
dan den touff gar kan ich nit daruß verston / sunder das du den Kindertouff
vnd den vnuerstand des Touffs verdammest   Waß das wasser bedütte doch . z.
wellind wir in diner vnd biblischer geschrift das besechen /   Deß Hinßen
bruder schribt du habest wider die fürsten geprediget das man sy mit der
kunst angriffen solte / ist eß war / oder so du krieg schirmen woltest / die tasten /
das gsang / oder anderß so nit in clarem wort findist / alß du diße gemelten /
stuk nit findest   So erman ich dich by gemeinem heil vnser allen welich dauon
abstan vnd allem gutdunken ich vnd hernach / So wirst du gar zin werden

der vns sunst in andern artiklen das gefalt den keiser in disem tütschen
ouch anderen länderen. So du dem Luther vnd hertzogen in die hand kumpst

lass die gemelten artikel fallen / vnd by den andern stand wie e im helde vnd
kempfer gottes / das stath in hast die bibel (darus Luther bibel babel
babel macht) zu schirm vnder das abgöttisch Luterisch schonen das er vnd
die glerten hirten by vns in aller welt gepflantzet hand / wider den
hinderlistigen hinlessigen glouben / wider ire predigung darin sy den cristen
nit lerend wie sy soltend / vnd aller welt eben das evangelium offetan

habend das sy leß selbs läsind # aber mit filen ... wan iederman höngt an irer
by vns ... sind mit zwentzig die dem wort gottes gloubind / nun den personen
Zwingli / ... vnd andere so anderstwo sind glert geachtet. Vnd ob du
darum liden müßtest / weist wol das es nit anders mag sin Cristus mus
noch mer liden in sinen glideren er aber wirt sy sterben vnd fest erhalten dich
zu dem end / Gott geb dir vnd vns gnad. Wan vnsere hirten sind ouch

also grim vnd wüttend wider vns scheltend ... vns buben an offenlicher
Cantzel # wir werdend ouch mit der zit sächen die verfolgung durch sy
über vns gan darin so bitt für vns by Gott. Nach ein mal manend wir
dich / vnd das darum / das wir dich vm der ... clarheit willen dines wortes
also hertzlich liebend vnd achtend / vnd vertruwt zu die getörend schriben

315 wellist nichts nach menschlichem gudt weder eigne oder fremddem handlen
leren oder verfechten / was geschricht ist widerumb niderwerffen / und wellist
allein gottes rechtes wort / vnd bruch / mitsampt der Regel Christi / vnuermischtem Touff vnd vnuermischtem nachtmal / wie wir in dem Ersten brief /
angerürt habend / vnd du bas bericht bist dan vnser hundert / verfechten
320 vnd leren ich vom so du vnd Carolstading / Jacobus strus / vnd Michel
Stifel mit gar rein zefliesen sin woltind (als ich aber vnd mine bruder hoffend
ir werdinds tün) were es wol ein ellend Euangelium in die welt
kumen Da aber sind wir einer weder vnsere hie vnd die zu Wittemberg
die vss einer Gschrift verkerung in die ander / vnd vss der blindtheit in andre
325 grössere täglich fallend Ich gloub vnd halt das Sy ware Bäpstler vnd
Bäpst werden wellind Jetz mit me Gott der herzüiger mit sinem sun
Jesu Christo vnserem heiland / vnd sine geist vnd wort sye mit dir vnd
vns allen Cünrat Grebel / andres Castelberg / felix mantz / Heinrich Aberli
Joannes panicellus / Hans ogsenfuss Hans Hudok
330 Die lantzman von Hall dine bruder / vnd siben nüw
Jung münzer dem Luther .

So dir fry nachgelaßen wirt / witer zepredigen vnd nichts begegnet
                                                    zů dem luther
wellend wir dir vnßers schribens Copy schiken vnd sin anthwort so er
vns widerschribt / wir habend in gemanet vnd vnßere die ouch / darmit
so es gott nit hinderen wurde / wellend wir iren mangel antzeigen
vnd nit fürchtn waß vns darum begegnet werde / Wir hand ouch sunst
kein Copy behalten den allein deß brieffs so wir zů Martino dinem wi-
derfächer geschriben habend / darum vernim vnßer myßert vnbehouen
schriben zů gůttem vff / vnd biß gwüß das wirß vß warer liebe getan
habind / wem wir sind mit / wort / vnd anfechtung vnd widersächeren
olich / wie wol du daß gelert vnd sterber / im geist . Vm diser gschrifft vnd wegen
willen habend wir gnůg mit dir gerett oder gschriben . Wellist vns
so es gott haben wil dine Ehesten grüßen vnd alle gemeindlich in eim
kurtzen brieff widerschriben / wirst du vns grosse fründ sand gemeinte
liebe zů dir erwecken

335
340
345

68

Der brief gehört
auch Doman Mün/
her zu

Zu altstetty
am Hartz

J. C. WENGER, a native of Honey Brook Township, Chester County, Pennsylvania, is Professor of Historical Theology in Goshen Biblical Seminary, Goshen, Indiana, a Mennonite institution. For decades he has devoted himself to the genesis and development of the Anabaptist-Mennonite tradition. He served as editor of the book, *They Met God,* and of *The Complete Writings of Menno Simons,* and is the author of *Even unto Death: The Heroic Witness of the Sixteenth-Century Anabaptists,* the *History of the Mennonites of the Franconia Conference, The Mennonites in Indiana and Michigan, Glimpses of Mennonite History and Doctrine, The Mennonite Church in America, The Doctrines of the Mennonites, Introduction to Theology, Separated unto God,* and *God's Word Written.* He has also served the Mennonites as a deacon, minister, and bishop, and as Vice-President for North America of the Mennonite World Conference. He received the BA degree from Goshen College, the MA in Philosophy from the University of Michigan, and the Doctorate in Theology from the University of Zürich. He also studied at the University of Basel, the University of Chicago, and at Westminster Theological Seminary, and was a postdoctoral Visiting Fellow at Princeton Theological Seminary. It is his hope that these letters of Conrad Grebel may contribute to a better understanding of Anabaptism and of its Swiss founder who died at 28 in 1526.